THE ART
OF STAYING
FOCUSED

A Guide to Overcoming
Distractions and Procrastination

Rose Jones

Table of Contents

Chapter 1

INTRODUCTION TO THE ART OF STAYING FOCUSED

Chapter 2

UNDERSTANDING DISTRACTIONS AND PROCRASTINATION

Chapter 3

THE POWER OF MINDFULNESS AND CONCENTRATION

Chapter 4

DEVELOPING MINDFULNESS AND CONCENTRATION TECHNIQUES

Chapter 5

THE IMPORTANCE OF SELF-CARE

Chapter 6

OVERCOMING PROCRASTINATION AND DISTRACTIONS

Chapter 1

INTRODUCTION TO THE ART OF STAYING FOCUSED

In today's world, distractions are everywhere. From notifications on our phones to the endless stream of social media, it can be difficult to stay focused and achieve our goals. The Art of Staying Focused is a comprehensive guide to overcoming distractions and procrastination, helping individuals develops the necessary skills and habits to achieve greater focus, productivity, and satisfaction in life.

The importance of staying focused in today's world cannot be overstated. With the rapid pace of technological advancements and the increasing demands of work and personal life, it has never been more important to stay focused and avoid distractions. This is especially true for those who work in fast-paced environments, where the ability to concentrate and make quick decisions is crucial.

The benefits of being focused and avoiding distractions are numerous. By staying focused, individuals can increase their productivity, reduce stress, and achieve their goals more efficiently. They can also develop a greater sense of purpose, as they are able to concentrate on the tasks that matter most.

In this book, readers will learn about the different types of distractions, the psychology behind procrastination, and how to develop mindfulness and concentration. They will also learn how to create a focused work environment, manage their time effectively, and overcome procrastination. By following the techniques and strategies outlined in this book, readers will be able to achieve a more focused, productive, and satisfying life.

With a comprehensive and practical approach, The Art of Staying Focused is a must-read for anyone looking to improve their focus, overcome distractions, and achieve their goals. Whether you are a student, entrepreneur, or simply someone looking to improve your focus, this book has something for everyone. So, let's dive in and discover the art of staying focused.

Chapter 2

UNDERSTANDING DISTRACTIONS AND PROCRASTINATION

In today's fast-paced and constantly connected world, distractions and procrastination are common obstacles that can prevent individuals from reaching their full potential. In order to overcome these challenges, it is important to first understand what they are and how they affect our lives. This chapter will define distractions and procrastination, explore the causes of these issues, and examine the consequences of being distracted and procrastinating.

Defining Distractions and Procrastination

Distractions refer to any external or internal factor that takes our focus away from the task at hand. These distractions can come from various sources, including social media, email, phone notifications, or even our own thoughts and emotions. In order to be productive and efficient, it is important to manage distractions and stay focused on the task at hand.

Procrastination, on the other hand, refers to the tendency to put off tasks or delay starting a task until later. This is often due to distractions or a lack of motivation.

Procrastination can take many forms; from avoiding tasks altogether to making excuses for why we cannot begin a task right now. This habit can be detrimental to our productivity and success, as it often results in missing deadlines and increased stress.

It is essential to understand the causes and consequences of distractions and procrastination in order to overcome these obstacles and reach our full potential. By understanding the different types of distractions and the psychology behind procrastination, individuals will be better equipped to overcome these challenges and achieve greater focus and productivity.

The Causes of Distractions and Procrastination

Distractions and procrastination can have various causes, including boredom, anxiety, lack of motivation or interest in the task, a feeling of overwhelming stress and fear of failure. Technology has also contributed to the increase in distractions, with constant access to the internet and social media. Additionally, some individuals may struggle with distractions and procrastination due to underlying mental health issues, such as attention deficit hyperactivity disorder (ADHD) or depression.

Understanding the Consequences of Being Distracted and Procrastinating

The consequences of being distracted and procrastinating can be far-reaching and damaging. For example, individuals who struggle with distractions may have trouble completing tasks on time and may miss important deadlines. Procrastination can lead to increased stress and anxiety, as tasks become increasingly difficult the longer they are put off.

In the workplace, distractions and procrastination can have significant negative impacts on one's life, leading to decreased productivity, lower quality work, and increased stress and anxiety. It can also lead to missed deadlines, decreased confidence, and a sense of disappointment and failure. Additionally, it can impact personal relationships, as procrastination can lead to missed opportunities or appointments.

Distractions and procrastination are two of the biggest challenges to staying focused in today's world.

Different Types of Distractions

Distractions can come in many forms, from physical distractions like noise or visual distractions like screens, to mental distractions like worry or anxiety. Some common forms of distractions include:

- **Digital distractions:** The rise of technology has led to an increase in digital distractions, such as notifications from social media, email, and other digital devices.

- **Physical distractions:** Physical distractions, such as noise or bright lights, can be especially disruptive to focus and productivity.

- **Mental distractions:** Mental distractions, such as worry, anxiety, or negative thoughts, can be difficult to overcome and can severely impact focus and productivity.

The Psychology behind Procrastination

Procrastination is a complex issue, rooted in psychological and emotional factors. Some common causes of procrastination include:

- **Fear of failure:** The fear of not being able to complete a task to the best of one's abilities can lead to procrastination.

- **Perfectionism:** The desire to achieve perfection can lead to excessive planning and overthinking, causing individuals to put off starting a task.

- **Lack of motivation:** When individuals are not motivated or engaged with a task, they may be more likely to procrastinate.

- **Disorganization:** A cluttered workspace or poor time-management skills can lead to feelings of overwhelm and cause individuals to procrastinate.

In the following chapters, we will examine various strategies for managing distractions, overcoming procrastination, and staying focused in today's fast-paced and connected world. We will explore how mindfulness and concentration can help individuals develop the skills necessary to stay focused and avoid distractions.

Chapter 3

THE POWER OF MINDFULNESS AND CONCENTRATION

In this chapter, we will explore the power of mindfulness and concentration as tools for overcoming distractions and procrastination. Mindfulness and concentration are key skills that can help individuals stay focused, reduce stress, and achieve greater productivity, satisfaction, and success in life.

Mindfulness: The Art of Being Present

Mindfulness is the practice of being present in the moment, fully engaged with one's thoughts, feelings, and experiences. It entails staying focused on the here and now without interruption or judgment. By practicing mindfulness, individuals can cultivate greater self-awareness and focus, reducing the impact of distractions and improving overall well-being.

Benefits of Mindfulness

Increased focus: Mindfulness helps individuals stay focused on the present moment, reducing the impact of distractions and increasing productivity. This is because it promotes greater self-awareness and attention to the present moment.

Reduced stress and anxiety: By allowing individuals to be present and fully engaged with their thoughts, feelings, and experiences, mindfulness can help to reduce stress and anxiety. This is because it promotes relaxation and calm, allowing individuals to better manage stress and anxiety.

Improved mental clarity: Mindfulness can help individuals to gain a clearer understanding of their thoughts and feelings, leading to improved mental clarity and overall well-being.

Better relationships: Mindfulness can help individuals to be more present in their relationships, leading to greater connection and satisfaction with friends, family, and colleagues.

Mindfulness can help individuals to overcome procrastination and distractions, by promoting greater focus and motivation. By becoming more aware of one's thoughts and feelings, individuals can identify and avoid procrastination triggers, leading to greater productivity and success.

Concentration: The Art of Focusing

Concentration is the ability to focus attention on a single task, idea, or experience, avoiding distractions and increasing productivity. By practicing concentration, individuals can develop greater focus and achieve their goals with greater ease and efficiency.

Benefits of Concentration

Increased productivity: Concentration helps individuals stay focused. By avoiding distractions, individuals can accomplish more in less time, freeing up time for other important activities. This will lead to increased productivity and achievement.

Better decision making: With greater focus, individuals are better equipped to make quick and accurate decisions, leading to better outcomes and success in both personal and professional life.

Better problem solving: By focusing on a single task, individuals can more effectively solve problems, leading to greater creativity and innovation.

Increased motivation: Concentration helps individuals to be more motivated and engaged with their work, leading to greater satisfaction and success.

Improved mental clarity: Staying focused and avoiding distractions can help to reduce stress and anxiety, resulting in improved mental clarity and overall well-being.

Better relationships: With increased focus and reduced stress, individuals are able to develop stronger, more meaningful relationships with friends, family, and colleagues.

Mindfulness and concentration are powerful tools for overcoming distractions and procrastination, helping individuals to stay focused, reduce stress, and achieve greater productivity, satisfaction, and success in life. In the next chapter, we will explore practical strategies for developing these skills and incorporating them into daily life.

Chapter 4

DEVELOPING MINDFULNESS AND CONCENTRATION TECHNIQUES

In this chapter, we will explore practical strategies for developing mindfulness and concentration skills, incorporating them into daily life, and overcoming distractions and procrastination.

Mindfulness Techniques

❖ **Meditation:** Meditation is a mindfulness practice that involves focusing on the present moment and allowing thoughts and feelings to pass by without judgment. This can be done by setting aside time each day for meditation, using guided meditations, or engaging in mindfulness-based stress reduction programs.

❖ **Mindful Breathing:** Mindful breathing is a simple and effective way to incorporate mindfulness into daily life. This can be done by taking slow-deep breaths, focusing on the breath, and releasing any tension or distractions.

❖ **Mindful Movement**: Mindful movement, such as yoga or tai chi, is a way to incorporate mindfulness into physical activity, promoting relaxation and self-awareness.

❖ **Mindful Eating:** Engaging in mindful eating, such as paying attention to the taste, texture, and sensations of food, can help individuals to overcome procrastination and distractions, by promoting greater focus and well-being. This can help individuals to slow down and enjoy the experience of eating, reducing distractions and promoting greater focus. This also improves digestion and overall health.

❖ **Mindful Listening:** Mindful listening involves paying attention to the sounds around us, from the rustle of leaves to the hum of traffic. This can help individuals to become more present and reduce distractions, leading to greater focus and concentration.

❖ **Mindful Thoughts:** Mindful thoughts involve paying attention to one's thoughts, without judgment or distraction. This can help individuals to become more aware of their thought patterns and reduce stress, leading to greater well-being.

❖ **Mindful Appreciation:** Mindful appreciation involves taking time to appreciate the good things in life, from the beauty of nature to the kindness of others. This can help individuals to become more grateful and increase overall happiness and well-being.

❖ **Mindful Task Completion:** Incorporating mindfulness into daily tasks, such as washing dishes or doing laundry, can help individuals to overcome procrastination and distractions, by promoting greater focus and motivation. By becoming more present in the moment and focusing on each step of the task, individuals can increase their productivity and achieve their goals.

❖ **Body Scan:** The body scan is a mindfulness technique that involves paying attention to each part of the body, starting from the toes and moving up to the head. This technique helps individuals to focus on the present moment, reducing stress and anxiety.

❖ **Sensory Awareness:** Sensory awareness involves paying attention to one's senses, such as sight, sound, touch, smell, and taste. This can be done by taking a few minutes to focus on a specific object, such as a flower or a tree, and noticing its color, shape, and texture.

❖ **Mindful Technology Use:** Incorporating mindfulness into technology use, such as setting aside specific times for checking email or social media, can help individuals to overcome procrastination and distractions, by promoting greater focus and motivation.

Incorporating mindfulness into daily life can be a powerful tool for overcoming procrastination and distractions, leading to greater focus and well-being. By practicing mindfulness in a variety of areas, such as meditation, mindful task completion, and mindful technology use, individuals can reduce stress and increase focus and motivation, leading to greater success and happiness. Additionally, incorporating mindfulness into daily life can lead to greater self-awareness, empathy, and compassion, promoting greater well-being for oneself and others.

Concentration Techniques

❖ **The Pomodoro Technique:** The Pomodoro Technique is a time-management technique that involves working in 25-minute intervals, with a 5-minute break in between. This technique helps individuals to focus on a single task for a set period of time, reducing distractions and increasing productivity.

❖ **The 80/20 Rule:** The 80/20 Rule states that 80% of results come from 20% of effort. This means that by focusing on the most important tasks first, individuals can achieve greater results with less effort.

- ❖ **Minimize Distractions:** Minimizing distractions is essential for effective concentration. This can involve creating a quiet workspace, minimizing notifications, or working in a place free from distractions.

  You might avoid having information disrupt a focused work flow by checking for it beforehand. On desktop and mobile devices, it could be a good idea to turn off all app alerts. Consider only responding to each request once daily and checking your inbox four times. Keeping control of your electronics may help you reduce distractions and increase focus.

- ❖ **Plan the previous evening:** List two things that must be accomplished for the day to be fruitful. Because the first one has a requirement or because it might take less time than expected, there are two possibilities. The backup task is the second one. Do these things first because waiting to accomplish them can easily ruin the start of any day. This includes checking emails, returning calls, and perusing social media.

- ❖ **Become at ease:** Every small business owner has a distinct interpretation of what this implies. Your level of comfort may vary depending on the setting in which you are working or dressed. You can keep focus throughout the workday by being aware of the surroundings that make you feel comfortable and concentrated at the same time.

❖ **Make use of meditation:** This may help your mind focus on one idea and let go of distracting ones. Consider beginning by sitting quietly for three to five minutes each day. Close your eyes and count to 34.

Since the mind has a tendency to wander to other ideas that can prevent you from reaching 34, this might be challenging at first. You can get back on track by just letting go of that notion without passing judgment on yourself and counting once again. When performing this exercise, take note of any feelings or sensations. Take your time; this is a harder chore than it first appears.

❖ **Smaller objectives:** Large goals may be effective in motivating audiences, but they may not aid in maintaining attention on the most crucial tasks. Take into account breaking down all objectives into manageable, smaller chunks. Therefore you might only need to concentrate for a shorter period of time, increasing your chances of finishing the activity.

❖ **Sleep:** People need seven to nine hours of sleep per night to maintain optimum health. Many owners of small businesses choose longer workdays over sleep in an effort to get more done.

Worst worse, this "sleep debt" can accumulate over an extended period of time. In fact, getting too little sleep may make it more difficult to maintain concentration and complete tasks to the best of your ability. Getting some sleep may help you become more focused and enhance your general health.

❖ **Go for a walk:** Standing up or, better still, leaving the office can help you concentrate more. Even a brief break from work can help the body and mind reenergize. When you come back from a break, it can assist you refocus on the subsequent work.

❖ **Disconnect and enjoy:** You can assist your brain focus later on a new activity by engaging in leisurely hobbies and screen time. Consider exercising, going for a run or bike ride, playing sports, completing puzzles, or playing chess for at least 30 minutes each day. A healthy body equals a good mind, always keep in mind. When the body is ill or the mind is depressed, it can be challenging to concentrate.

Developing mindfulness and concentration skills is essential for overcoming distractions and procrastination, and achieving greater focus, productivity, and satisfaction in life. Additionally, the practice of mindfulness can improve overall well-being and increase happiness, leading to greater satisfaction and fulfillment.

Chapter 5

THE IMPORTANCE OF SELF-CARE

In this chapter, we will explore the importance of self-care in reducing distractions and procrastination, and improving overall well-being.

The Benefits of Self-Care

o **Reduced Stress:** Self-care can help individuals to reduce stress and improve overall well-being. This can involve activities such as exercise, mindfulness, or taking time for hobbies and interests.

o **Increased Energy:** Self-care can help individuals to increase energy, focus, and motivation. This can involve activities such as sleep, eating a balanced diet, or taking breaks to recharge and refresh.

o **Improved Mental Health:** Self-care can help individuals to improve their mental health, reducing stress and anxiety. This can involve activities such as mindfulness, therapy, or engaging in hobbies and interests.

Self-Care Strategies

- o **Exercise:** Exercise is an essential component of self-care, helping individuals to reduce stress, increase energy, and improve overall well-being.

- o **Mindfulness:** Mindfulness is a powerful tool for reducing stress and improving mental health, making it an important component of self-care.

- o **Hobbies and Interests:** Engaging in hobbies and interests can help individuals to reduce stress, improve mental health, and achieve greater satisfaction and fulfillment.

Self-care is essential for reducing distractions and procrastination, and improving overall well-being. By incorporating self-care into daily life, individuals can achieve greater focus, energy, and satisfaction, leading to greater success and fulfillment.

Chapter 6

OVERCOMING PROCRASTINATION AND DISTRACTIONS

In this chapter, we will explore practical strategies for overcoming procrastination and distractions, leading to greater focus and success.

Every business owner and leader should work on their abilities to overcome distractions and maintain focus. Your capacity for maintaining attention and controlling distractions will determine whether or not you have a productive day.

You are constantly surrounded by diversions. If anything, you will have more distractions to deal with. One of the best things you can do for yourself if you want to accomplish your goals is to learn how to deal with distractions and procrastination.

You can avoid distractions and procrastination and do your most critical job each day with careful preparation and conscious time management.

Strategies for Overcoming Procrastination and Distractions

> **Prioritization:** Prioritizing tasks and setting specific goals can help individuals to overcome procrastination, by providing a clear direction and focus. This can be done by creating a to-do list, using a calendar, or setting clear goals.

> **Time Management:** Effective time management, including setting aside specific times for focused work, can help individuals to overcome procrastination, by reducing distractions and promoting greater focus.

Switching between tasks makes it simple to become sidetracked. Get your thoughts to concentrate on only one task at a time to avoid distractions. To avoid distractions, schedule key tasks and then set aside time to do them.

For anything good to be accomplished, dedicated time is required. Establish a deadline for finishing the task after being clear on the outcome you wish to attain. When you can concentrate on one item and maintain that focus, staying focused is simpler.

> **Set a shorter deadline for yourself:** Working longer hours does not always equate to getting more done. Parkinson's law is that "work tends to

increase to occupy the time we have available for its completion." And the issue is, we usually occupy our free time with activities that are distracting. This is due to the fact that our minds are programmed to save energy wherever possible. There is a good probability we won't do something if we don't have to. Instead, we will let ourselves become engrossed in a YouTube video or a smartphone game.

But, when a deadline is approaching, we suddenly become laser-focused and avoid all distractions at all costs. You will come up with a solution to complete a task once you are aware that it must be completed.

Give yourself less time to complete the task to reduce distractions. This is similar to setting a fictitious deadline for yourself, but it comes with a real consequence. Inform your client or your manager that you will deliver a project draft to them by the end of the day. Pick a partner who will hold you accountable for sticking to your deadline. Whichever method you use, establishing a strict deadline will enable you to stay focused and increase your production.

➢ **Make advance plans:** If you don't have a clear plan for your day, it's simple to become sidetracked. Make planning an integral part of your workday to avoid distractions. So that you know exactly where to spend your time on a Monday morning, plan your week on a Friday or Sunday.

By doing this, you can avoid being sidetracked to start the week. Making a plan for the following day can help you wake up with a clear head.

➢ **Establish daily targets**: Establish daily goals to help you stay focused and overcome distractions. Simplifying your day to include only the most important tasks will prevent you from becoming sidetracked when you have a lot going on.

You might divide up those daily objectives into smaller chores to make it easier for you to focus. Completing a limited number of daily objectives increases motivation and guarantees that you conclude the day feeling successful and forward-moving.

➢ **Every day, choose three overarching goals:** Choose three tasks that must be completed for your day to be fruitful. A big list of tasks can seem overwhelming and leave us feeling unmanageable. When we are prepared to give up before we even begin, it is simple to succumb to distractions. By setting three goals for yourself each day, you can make up for it. When you look up from your work, post the sticky notes where you can see them every time.

You will have a clear understanding of what you need to work on by reducing the amount of daily goals. When working on those chores, you will be more focused and less likely to get distracted.

Every morning, ask yourself: What are the three most crucial tasks I need to get done today? Put all additional items on a different to-do list. As soon as you've completed the first three objectives, you can start working on those less crucial jobs.

➤ **Breaking Tasks into Smaller Parts:** Breaking tasks into smaller, manageable steps makes them less intimidating, reducing the temptation to procrastinate. This can be done by creating a step-by-step plan, or using a productivity app.

➤ **Set a Timer:** Setting a timer helps individuals to focus on a task for a set period of time, reducing the temptation to procrastinate. This can be done using a timer app.

➤ **Maintain a purposeful focus:** If you want to reduce distractions, start approaching everything you do with intention. When you are deliberate, you have a clear vision of what you want to accomplish in any circumstance.

Because you have specified it up front, this intentionality helps you maintain your attention on the goals you want to attain. Focus is improved by eliminating distractions and being purposeful.

➤ **Use visual cues:** Fix visual cues at strategic locations. For instance, you may stick a straightforward standing panel on top of your business desk with the two words "No Distraction" written on it loudly. Seeing this reminder and saying it out loud will help you concentrate when you have trouble staying on task or want to break from it to check email or social media. This hint is quite useful.

➤ **Get an Accountability Partner:** Getting an accountability partner can help individuals to stay motivated and avoid procrastination. This can be done by partnering with a friend, family member, or colleague who holds them accountable for their goals and progress.

➤ **Eliminate the Distractions:** Eliminating distractions, such as turning off notifications, closing irrelevant tabs, or working in a quiet environment, can help individuals to overcome distractions and increase focus.

Start forming routines that will help you avoid distractions and make sure you stay focused in order to break the distraction behaviors. Examine the routines you follow that make you feel or become distracted. After that, begin removing each distraction one at a time.

This might require an hour-earlier start to the workday, taking a break for lunch, exercising or meditating throughout the day. Although it may seem easy to change habits, doing so requires dedication. But even a minor adjustment can make a tremendous difference.

➢ **Keep an eye out for daydreaming:** The majority of our waking hours are spent thinking about things other than our obligations. In part to save ourselves the effort of having to focus, we are operating on autopilot and our minds are roaming. The secret to increased productivity is to become aware of mental distractions and refocus your concentration on the activity at hand.

This entails being aware of your thoughts and noticing when your attention begins to wander. This enables you to control your focus and refocus your attention when you falter. You consciously stop this diversion rather than allowing yourself to keep wandering over to social media to check your newsfeed.

Keep an eye out for distractions that are particularly difficult to ignore so you can spot them earlier. Take a deep breath and make the decision not to react when you are tempted to give in to a distraction. It's more difficult to get yourself back on track after giving in and allowing yourself to focus on anything else, like reading emails.

In other words, pay attention to your ideas rather than allowing your attention to drift from one thing to another.

> **Creating a Work Environment:** Creating a work environment that is free from distractions and promotes focus, such as a dedicated workspace or a quiet library, can help individuals to overcome distractions and increase productivity.

Start forming routines that will enable you to block out distractions and maintain your attention. Start by setting up an environment that makes it harder for you to become distracted from what you are working on. Doing this is not always simple. One reason is that many of us rely on computers to complete our tasks, but we also use them to access the internet, which provides us with our biggest sources of distraction. Try utilizing a website blocker app if you frequently find yourself straying over to video or retail websites.

Develop routines that let others and yourself know that you are free from distractions. Your office door should be shut. Put on earbuds that block out noise. Move your phone away from you (so you can't readily pick it up) and turn it off or put it on mute. You might find it useful to relocate to a more quiet area if you work in an open office. According to studies, we are stopped by people more frequently and distractions occur 64 percent more frequently in open offices.

Avoid multitasking and get rid of as many distractions and justifications as you can to focus only on one activity at a time.

➢ **Taking Regular Breaks:** Taking regular breaks, such as stepping away from the computer or going for a walk, can help individuals to overcome distractions and increase focus.

Regular breaks are crucial for reducing distractions and maintaining attention. You must take breaks to maintain high levels of motivation and energy if you want to produce greater and better results.

You can retain your focus and be more productive when you take regular breaks. By taking breaks, you can avoid being sidetracked while working on your most crucial tasks.

➢ **Create a game out of it to exercise your brain**: Your mind is similar to a muscle. You must develop it if you want to use it well. By steadily improving our focus, we may teach our brains to remain concentrated. This will improve our capacity for sustained concentration.

You could, for instance, set a timer and dedicate a certain amount of uninterrupted time—say, 45 minutes—to a particular work. After that, take a 15-minute pause.

If 45 minutes is too long for you, start with something shorter—say, 25 minutes—and then take a five-minute rest. Turn it into a game by challenging yourself to finish your assignment quickly before the timer goes off. Then, for a set period of time, give yourself permission to indulge in any form of diversion.

Following the break, work continues until the timer goes off. The amount of work you can accomplish using this technique will astound you!

➢ **Take on more challenging work:** If you frequently become sidetracked and have difficulties focusing, it's possible that your job isn't entirely engrossing you. It's likely that, despite the fact that you may feel as though you have been working hard all day, your mind is simply trying to pass the time by thinking of more interesting things to do.

Difficult tasks need more working memory and concentration, which leaves us with less mental ability to wander to the closest engaging diversion. When our abilities are pushed, we are most likely to attain a state of total job immersion. When our abilities significantly surpass the requirements of our jobs, such as when we spend hours mindlessly entering data, we become bored.

Analyze the amount of busywork you are doing that is not productive. Do you find it difficult to become invested in the project? This can suggest that you are capable of handling tasks that are more difficult. We can become engrossed and overly preoccupied with the task when we take on more challenging work that tests our knowledge and intellectual capabilities. Our brains are programmed to concentrate on something new, enjoyable, or dangerous. And doing these things makes us feel accomplished.

With a task we consider to be mundane, we lack this sensation of accomplishment.

➢ **Stop the stress and distraction cycle**: Stress can also have a significant impact on our inability to concentrate or block out distractions. We attempt to work far too frequently despite feeling overburdened. As a result, we become flustered, worn out, easily distracted, and unable to concentrate. Being easily distracted may be a sign that you are experiencing high levels of stress.

Even a term has been given to it: "easily distracted anxiety." These signs include:

> You have trouble staying focused, and your thoughts frequently stray from what you were paying attention to.
> You have more trouble than usual remaining on task and organizing your thoughts.
> You have confusion and deteriorated thinking.
> Your short-term memory seems to be less effective than usual.

Controlling your tension will make it easier for you to restore your attention and ignore distractions. You need to learn techniques for body and mind relaxation if you want to lessen your body's reaction to stress. Ensure that you receive enough rest. Find techniques to manage your anxiety by doing breathing exercises.

> **Use Technology:** Technology can be a powerful tool for overcoming distractions and increasing productivity. This can involve using productivity apps, such as Trello or Todoist, or utilizing tools

that help to block distracting websites, such as Freedom or Cold Turkey.

➢ **Self-Discipline:** Developing self-discipline can help individuals to overcome procrastination and distractions, by promoting greater focus and motivation. This can include setting specific goals, sticking to a routine, and avoiding procrastination triggers.

➢ **Positive Self-Talk:** Encouraging positive self-talk and avoiding negative self-criticism can help individuals to overcome procrastination and distractions, by promoting greater self-esteem and motivation.

➢ **Reward System:** Implementing a reward system, such as rewarding oneself for completing tasks or reaching specific goals, can help individuals to overcome procrastination and distractions, by increasing motivation and focus.

Delaying pleasure might really aid people in concentrating on a task at hand. As a direct motivator, pick the work and the personalized reward (eating, checking social media, calling a buddy, etc.) before beginning.

➢ **Seeking Support:** Seeking support from friends, family, or a therapist can help individuals to overcome procrastination and distractions, by providing encouragement and accountability.

In order to overcome distractions and procrastination, it is important to recognize the patterns and triggers that cause these habits. This can involve self-reflection and analyzing one's personal habits and behaviors, as well as taking a critical look at the environment in which one works and lives.

For example, individuals who find themselves constantly checking their phone for notifications may want to consider setting specific times for checking their device or disabling notifications during work hours. Those who are prone to procrastination may want to break down tasks into smaller, more manageable steps, or prioritize their to-do list to focus on the most important tasks first.

It is also important to recognize that distractions and procrastination can be symptoms of deeper issues, such as stress, anxiety, or burnout. In these cases, it may be necessary to seek professional help, such as counseling or therapy, in order to address the underlying causes and develop effective strategies for overcoming distractions and procrastination.

In conclusion, procrastination and distractions can have a significant negative impact on one's life, leading to decreased productivity and well-being. However, by incorporating the strategies outlined in this guide, individuals can overcome procrastination and distractions, leading to greater focus and success. By becoming more mindful and taking a proactive approach to time management, individuals can achieve their goals and lead a more fulfilling life. Additionally, seeking support from others can help individuals to stay on track and achieve their goals, leading to a more fulfilling life.

It's simple to become sidetracked at work with everything going on. Try any of these suggestions if you want to maintain your focus and avoid distractions. You can be more productive and get more done in less time if you can cut out distractions from your workday.

www.ingramcontent.com/pod-product-compliance
Lightning Source LLC
Chambersburg PA
CBHW070318240526
45467CB00046B/1998